Merry Christmas 1991
  to Bill & Lillian

≡ Love — from Evelyn.

Pittsburgh

THEN AND NOW

Pittsburgh

THEN AND NOW

Arthur G. Smith

University of Pittsburgh Press

Published by the University of Pittsburgh Press, Pittsburgh, Pa. 15260
Copyright © 1990, University of Pittsburgh Press
All rights reserved
Baker & Taylor International, London
Printed in Japan

Library of Congress Cataloging-in-Publication Data

Smith, Arthur G.
  Pittsburgh then and now / Arthur G. Smith.
    p. cm.
  ISBN 0-8229-3830-8.
  1. Pittsburgh (Pa.)—History—Pictorial works. 2. Pittsburgh
(Pa.)—Description—Views. I. Title.
F159.P643S65 1990
974.8′86—dc20

                            89-35895
                              CIP

Contents

Pittsburgh: Continuity and Change

Through the ages one of the characteristics that has attracted people to cities is their dynamic quality. They are places of diverse human activity and, despite the continuity that results from a given physical and cultural environment, they are places of constant change. Such has certainly been the case with Pittsburgh as it evolved from frontier village to busy commercial town to industrial city to modern postindustrial metropolis, all in the historically brief span of two hundred years. Photography covers only the second half of that history, but it provides many vivid images of this city as its citizens struggled to create a livable environment amidst the consequences of remarkable industrial productivity.

What was it like to live in Pittsburgh one hundred, seventy-five, or fifty years ago? We have various written records that describe that experience, and we treasure these historic documents. However, we do not always give similar value to old photographs, which can also provide vivid glimpses of the past—impressions that are seldom matched in their precision and accuracy by verbal descriptions. There are 161 old photographs in this book. Forty-eight of them were taken during the twenty-five years before 1910 and 87 between 1920 and 1939, constituting the greatest concentration of "then" images.

In 1868 James Parton wrote in *The Atlantic Monthly* that looking down upon Pittsburgh from one of its hilltops was like looking into "hell with the lid taken off." This damning description was repeated by Lincoln Steffens and others around the turn of the century. The remarkable transformation implied by Rand McNally's selection of Pittsburgh as "the most livable city in the United States" in 1985 is illustrated in some of these photographic comparisons, particularly the ones that focus upon earlier industrial activity. The city—its rivers, buildings, and air—is cleaner than it was one hundred, or fifty years ago. The return of trees to the hillsides, once wooded and subsequently denuded of foliage, has made their appearance more picturesque. Only those who are unwavering in their nostalgic commitment to the past would claim that downtown Pittsburgh today, with its mix of elegant old and stylish new buildings, is not a far more pleasant and visually satisfying Golden Triangle than existed fifty years ago.

Yet it is also evident that the changes of the past century are not all improvements, at least in aesthetic terms. Between "then" and "now" many buildings have deteriorated and become less attractive in appearance, while others have disappeared, replaced by structures which may be more functional, but are less pleasing to the eye. For instance, one need only view the dreary mediocrity of many of the post–World War II apartment houses along Fifth Avenue in Shadyside and recall the strikingly individualistic mansions that once graced "Millionaires' Row" to realize the perils of urban change that is more concerned with function than with appearance. One hundred years ago many buildings in Pittsburgh were adorned with elegant features that are now either no longer in vogue or too expensive to reproduce or maintain. We are all poorer for at least some of the changes that are illustrated in these comparative photographs.

This is essentially a book of record, however, not of interpretation. Social scientists, from historians to anthropologists, may use it in pursuit of various theories of urban development and the adjustment of people to a demanding environment. For others it will be a record of urban change—from architectural styles that reflected turn-of-the-century eclecticism to the more recent styles labeled "modernist" and "postmodernist"; from horse to streetcar to automobile, each determining changes in living patterns; from steel mills to skeletal ruins along the Monongahela River, documenting the demise of the industry that made this city famous—or infamous. Yet for many who grew up in or near Pittsburgh, it will be a measure of their own past. Memories are evoked by means of various artifacts, including old letters and mementoes, but perhaps no reminders are more precise and evocative than old photographs. For many of us these photographs are the backdrop of our childhood, and we will measure family and personal changes against the setting of this changing city.

This book and the archives of Western Pennsylvania owe much to the skill and diligence of the photographers of the past whose work is shown here. I have acknowledged each of them whenever possible. Without the magnificent photographic collections of the Pennsylvania Room in the Carnegie Library of

Pittsburgh, the Archives of Industrial Society in the University of Pittsburgh's Hillman Library, and the Historical Society of Western Pennsylvania, our sense of Pittsburgh's past would be much less rich.

I offer a grateful thank-you to Frank J. Kurtik, associate curator of the Archives of Industrial Society in the Hillman Library, and Maria Zini, head of the Pennsylvania Department of the Carnegie Library of Pittsburgh. They have been especially helpful in providing access to photographs from the rich collections over which they preside. A glance at the photographic credits at the end of this book reveals how heavily I have relied upon these two sources. I give a special thank-you to Patti Gordon, a professional photographer, whose skills in the Chatham College photo lab are reflected in the quality of the photographs in this book. Most of the negatives were good, but some were not. That did not deter her from making some pictures that are far better than their negatives. She has the ability to make a silk purse out of a sow's ear, photographically speaking. While on the subject of photography, I am grateful to Robert J. Cooley, director of media resources at Chatham College, for his professional assistance with various phases of this book and to the Central Research Fund of Chatham College for funding the early photographic expenses involved. I also offer a collective thank-you to the building managers who gave me access to the roofs and upper stories of their buildings so that I could duplicate the viewpoint of earlier photographs.

My own contribution has been one of persistence in finding the photographs of the past and in taking photographs of the present from the precise camera position of the original. Occasionally this was not possible because of the demolition of buildings, or—more happily—the growth of trees that now obstruct the view. In these cases, I have photographed from the closest available approximation of the original camera position. In a few instances the scenes are so extensively altered that I had to approximate the comparisons without common points of reference. The process of putting together the materials of this book was both a challenge and a joy. My hope is that the reader will derive some of the same pleasure from viewing this book that I did from creating it.

ARTHUR G. SMITH
Professor of History
Chatham College

PITTSBURGH

Then and Now

THE TRIANGLE

Circa 1920

■ Geography has played an important role in the development of Pittsburgh. The Allegheny and Monongahela rivers and the bluff on which Duquesne University is located historically defined the bounds of the central business district, called the Triangle, and imposed fixed limits upon outward expansion. Faced with these constraints and the growing demand for downtown office space,

Pittsburgh's turn-of-the-century real estate developers seized upon the new concept of the skyscraper, a tall, steel-framed, elevator-equipped building. By the end of the first decade of this century, Pittsburgh had become a city noted for its numerous skyscrapers. That trend has continued into the 1980s, the new skyscrapers dwarfing their older counterparts.

The Triangle, seen from Mt. Washington. This is probably the most photographed view of Pittsburgh—and before photography, the most painted and sketched view. Pittsburgh is one of few cities where the skyscrapers can be photographed from above while the photographer stands on the ground.

The upper Triangle with the Smithfield Street Bridge in the foreground. The tallest structure in 1898 was the tower of the County Courthouse, which by 1986 was almost lost amid the surrounding skyscrapers. The dark building to its left is the Carnegie Building, the first of Pittsburgh's skyscrapers to have both a fireproof steel frame and elevators. It was completed in 1895 and demolished in 1952 to make way for the expansion of Kaufmann's department store.

Only four years separated this and the previous old photo-graph, yet several new skyscrapers had been added. The Frick Building can be seen next to the Carnegie Building and towering over it—probably a calculated affront, since by 1901 Henry Clay Frick and Andrew Carnegie were no longer on speaking terms. The building boom in the downtown at the turn of the century, a consequence of the great wealth generated by local industry, continued until the outbreak of World War I.

The Grant Building is prominent on the right and the Koppers and Gulf buildings stand side by side near the center of the picture. All three were built between 1926 and 1933 and dominated the Pittsburgh skyline for twenty years thereafter. They were also the last masonry skyscrapers with partially load-bearing walls constructed in Pittsburgh.

Conspicuous in 1986 and clustered in the center of the photograph are, from left to right, Number Three Mellon Bank Center (1949–52, forty-one stories), the USX Tower (1969–71, sixty-four stories), and One Oxford Center (1982–83, forty-six stories).

The lower Triangle. These photographs were taken from the top of the Gulf Building. The earlier one shows the three recently constructed Gateway Towers near the Point; by 1987 the Oliver Plaza buildings, Fifth Avenue Place, and the CNG Tower obstructed the view of the Point. There have been more tall buildings constructed along Liberty Avenue since 1955, as the skyscraper trend in the downtown has been extended to the Allegheny River side of the Triangle.

THE POINT

1908

■ During the first half of this century the Point, at the confluence of the Allegheny and Monongahela rivers, was primarily a freight terminal for the Pennsylvania Railroad, the transfer point between the rail traffic from the East and the river traffic from the West. The dramatic conversion to its present state began after World War II when it became the centerpiece for the first Pittsburgh Renaissance. The Point and the adjacent land that constituted the precincts of Fort Pitt eventually became a state park. After the razing of the old buildings, almost two decades passed before the project was completed. Beyond the park, Gateway Center, with its sleek skyscrapers and elegant plaza, completed the Renaissance improvements at the Point, making a dramatic statement of confidence in Pittsburgh's future at a time when living conditions and environmental pollution were causing many businessmen and corporate executives to think seriously about moving elsewhere.

Prior to 1929, when the river system was opened to year-round navigation, it was common practice to collect barges loaded with coal along the Monongahela waterfront until the water level rose sufficiently to permit them to proceed safely down the Ohio. Sometimes the river was so congested that one could almost cross it by jumping from barge to barge. The long buildings on the left, along the Allegheny waterfront, are Exposition Hall and Machinery Hall. Until 1916 they served as the sites of annual displays of the latest in industrial products. These expositions, which attracted large crowds, were the urban counterparts of the traditional agricultural fairs held throughout the United States. Exposition Hall survived until the end of the 1940s, as revealed in the next photograph, but by that time its large display space was being used to accommodate automobiles impounded by the city.

THE POINT

1947

The contrast between then and now dramatically illustrates
the achievement of the Renaissance project which began
shortly after the earlier photograph was taken. The Point
had long since ceased to serve as an important transfer depot
from rail to water, and the railroad storage facilities were
easily moved elsewhere.

THE POINT

The Point Bridge and the Manchester Bridge, seen on the left and right-center of this 1939 photograph, were major traffic arteries from the south and north sides of the rivers. They converged at the Point, from which traffic came and went via the Water Street ramp (on the left). This limited access to two major bridges provided a splendid opportunity for serious traffic congestion every weekday morning and afternoon. This area is now part of Point State Park.

The earlier photograph was taken fifteen years after the Point Park project was begun. Two major impediments to its completion were the old bridges which remained while city, county, and state officials debated which governing body would bear the considerable expense involved in removing them.

■ As long as the rivers were a principal means of transportation for goods carried to and from the city, commercial activity in Pittsburgh centered upon the Monongahela Wharf. This continued well into the twentieth century despite the competition of railroads and highways. The wharf was a busy place, with passengers and freight arriving and departing via the river system which stretched for nineteen hundred miles to the west and south. The wharf subsequently became a convenient place for commuters to park their cars, with a vehicular capacity far greater than today. The transformation of the waterfront to its present state was begun before World War II. In 1939 Robert Moses, a highly regarded city planner, issued an "Arterial Plan for Pittsburgh," including in his recommenda-

tions the creation of Fort Duquesne Boulevard—a crosstown boulevard linking the bridges at the Point with Penn and Liberty avenues beyond the downtown—and a parkway running east along the Monongahela, then inland to Wilkinsburg. His goal was to alleviate traffic congestion in the central city by enabling traffic passing through town to avoid downtown streets, while improving access to the city from its eastern suburbs. The reconstruction of both the Monongahela and Duquesne wharves was the result of subsequent efforts to implement these recommendations. Fort Pitt Boulevard along the Monongahela was built before the outbreak of the war in 1941, creating a city bypass for traffic crossing the Point and Manchester bridges. By then the wharf's commercial function had practically ceased.

THE MONONGAHELA WHARF

March 1987

In the nineteenth century, riverboats were a common sight along the shore, with considerable movement and storage of goods nearby. The 1987 photograph shows Fort Pitt Boulevard, with parking space below.

Because of the rise and fall of the river level, which was much more pronounced before a system of dams and locks was constructed after World War II to diminish the danger of floods, the waterfront was served by floating docks. Steamboats tied up to these docks, and goods and passengers were transferred through them to the wharf.

200 block of Water Street (Fort Pitt Boulevard). This single block of buildings, dating primarily from the 1870s, is all that remains of the nineteenth-century Water Street commercial frontage.

Seen from the Smithfield Street Bridge ramp. The bridge in the upper left of the earlier photograph is the Wabash Bridge, which was torn down in 1947 to make way for the changes near the Point.

THE MONONGAHELA WHARF

Circa 1925

Boats continued to use the wharf through the 1930s,
although commercial steamboat traffic steadily diminished
between the wars.

With the decrease in commercial activity, the automobile
began to invade the wharf in the 1920s. The parking lot
provided more space for cars than it does today.

Water Street (Fort Pitt Boulevard) looking east from number 209. These buildings probably survived because of the decline in commercial activity at the wharf and the construction of the Boulevard of the Allies in the 1920s. The boulevard tended to separate Water Street and First Avenue from the busier parts of the downtown, making it a less desirable business location.

■ Pittsburgh grew first along the Monongahela River; development on the Allegheny side of the Triangle came much later. The Duquesne Wharf never had the commercial prominence of its Monongahela counterpart. The Allegheny River flowed more swiftly and its riverbank was steeper, making loading and unloading of goods more difficult. Between 1904 and the late 1940s the Duquesne Wharf's primary function was to provide passage for the railroad from Union Station to the freight yards at the Point.

Downriver from the Seventh Street Bridge. The Duquesne Wharf, like the Monongahela Wharf, adapted to the age of the automobile. Cars were parked down to the water's edge beyond the next bridge, but since the nearer portion of the wharf was steeper and unpaved, the possibility of losing one's vehicle to the river was sufficient to deter additional parking. The three buildings in the foreground remain with little apparent alteration.

August 1987

Upriver from the Seventh Street Bridge. Since the railroad did not provide passenger service to the Point, it is probable that the track was used as a siding for passenger cars that were not in service. By 1932 freight traffic to the Point may have been infrequent.

From the Ninth Street Bridge. The railroad, which dominated the waterfront in 1932, has been replaced by the automobile.

THE DUQUESNE WHARF

February 1987

Fort Duquesne Boulevard from Eighth Street toward Tenth Street. The only common point of reference is the Pennsylvania Railroad bridge in the background. The earlier photograph shows the street about to be paved with granite blocks, the predominant paving material in Pittsburgh during the first four decades of this century.

■ The streets in the Triangle were surveyed and laid out by Colonel George Woods in 1784. Not often is the surveyor honored by having a street named after him, but then Colonel Woods did the naming. He was also responsible for the triangulation of various downtown intersections, thereby creating severe traffic problems through the years. One way in which the composition and appearance of the downtown has changed in the most recent half century is that masonry has been replaced by steel as the principal building material. This change, combined with the predominance of the International Style of architecture from the 1950s through the 1970s, has produced buildings that are taller, sleeker, and less ornate than their predecessors. Mies van der Rohe and other arbiters of that style were uncompromising in their rejection of all ornament that did not have a practical use: they believed that "form follows function." The result was a great proliferation of buildings that were cheap to construct and easy to maintain, but had a bland monotony in appearance compared with the more ornate buildings that they replaced. Fortunately there are still plenty of those older buildings in Pittsburgh to add spice to the mixture. In the 1980s numerous "postmodernist" skyscrapers have added diversity to the architecture of the downtown.

Liberty Avenue northeast from Sixth Street. Until 1904 the Pennsylvania Railroad ran freight trains down the middle of Liberty Avenue, no doubt causing considerable traffic problems on one of Pittsburgh's busiest streets.

Intersection of Liberty Avenue and Grant Street seen from the top of the Union Station. These two photographs of the same scene, taken eighty years apart, make an eloquent argument for the proposition that change is the predominant theme in the urban environment, at least in the central city.

They also show that there is a higher density of working population in the city today than at the turn of the century. Skyscrapers hold more people than do buildings of only a few stories.

Grant Street southwest from Fifth Avenue. The Frick Building replaced the cluster of buildings on Grant Street, including the church, in 1901. St. Peter's Episcopal Church, built in 1852, is a splendid example of an historically correct neo-Gothic building, modeled after numerous fourteenth-century English parish churches. When Henry Clay Frick bought the land, he gave the church to its parishioners, most of whom by then lived in the eastern suburbs of Oakland and Shadyside. They had the good sense to dismantle it and reconstruct it on the corner of Forbes and Craft avenues in Oakland, where it still stands today.

Allegheny County Courthouse, Grant Street between Fifth and Forbes avenues. The courthouse was designed by Henry Hobson Richardson and built in 1884–88. The substantial staircase that leads to the main entrance was added in 1913 after the removal of the top of Grant's Hill lowered the level of the street. In 1928, when Grant Street was widened, the stairs were removed and the entry portals elongated; what had been an underground story of the building became the main entrance. Next to the courthouse is the City-County Building, built in 1915–17.

Smithfield Street northeast across the Boulevard of the Allies. Smithfield Street offers an interesting combination of the old and the new. The west side of the street (left) contains numerous buildings that date from before World War I.

Smithfield Street, east side, northeast from the Boulevard of the Allies. The east side of the street between the Boulevard of the Allies and Sixth Avenue was built predominantly after World War II. The extravagant, castlelike building on the far left was the Old Post Office, which was built in the 1880s and demolished in 1966.

Smithfield Street, northeast from Third Avenue. Many of
the changes that appear on the west side of the street (left)
were made shortly after 1905.

Smithfield Street, west side, southwest from number 109.
The blocks south of the Boulevard of the Allies have been altered less than the other parts of the street. The store fronts have changed, along with their proprietors, but many of the buildings are the same as they were in 1926.

Smithfield Street from Seventh Avenue to Liberty Avenue.
A cluster of buildings which were built in the second half of
the nineteenth century has survived at the north end of
Smithfield Street. The building on the left occupies one of
the triangular-shaped lots created by George Woods's street
plan. It was constructed in the 1880s, with cast-iron
embellishments on the ground floor.

View of Wood Street and large buildings, PITTSBURGH, P.A.

Wood Street. The prominent building on the right in each photograph was originally the Farmers' Deposit National Bank Building. Its exterior was remodeled in 1967 to reflect changes in architectural tastes and building materials since it was constructed in 1903. It is now identified as 301 Fifth Avenue.

Sixth Avenue from Liberty Avenue.
Unlike the comparable intersection
at Seventh and Liberty avenues (see
pp. 58–59), here the ornate triangular
building has disappeared, but the
Granite Building and Duquesne Club
beyond it, newly built in 1890, have
survived.

Fifth Avenue from Liberty Avenue. This intersection of a century ago displays some of the less memorable buildings of that era. Their replacements are not notably distinguished either.

Fifth Avenue above Wood Street. These views of Fifth
Avenue reveal that in this block the scale and miscellaneous
quality of the facades have changed little in eighty-five years.

The Diamond Market. The Diamond Market House filled Market Square until it was demolished in 1961. Its two separate buildings spanned Diamond Street and were connected by an elevated footbridge over Market Street.

Diamond Street looking northwest under the Diamond Market. The view across Market Square was very different in 1933 from what it is today. The arches of the Market House gave the area an interesting, three-dimensional quality with changing patterns of light and dark. Brick pavement, grass, trees, and park benches have transformed this space into a popular recreational site. Occasionally it serves as the gathering place for public events.

Northeast corner of Diamond Street at Market Square.
From the time Pittsburgh was a frontier village until the mid-twentieth century, Market Square was a principal market-place of the city, the site of a succession of market houses surrounded by wholesale and retail shops. By the 1930s shopping possibilities had been spread more evenly through-out the downtown and established neighborhoods, while post-World War II Pittsburgh has experienced the prolifera-tion of suburban shopping centers—a consequence of the widespread use of automobiles. Although it is still possible to shop in Market Square, more serious shopping is now done elsewhere.

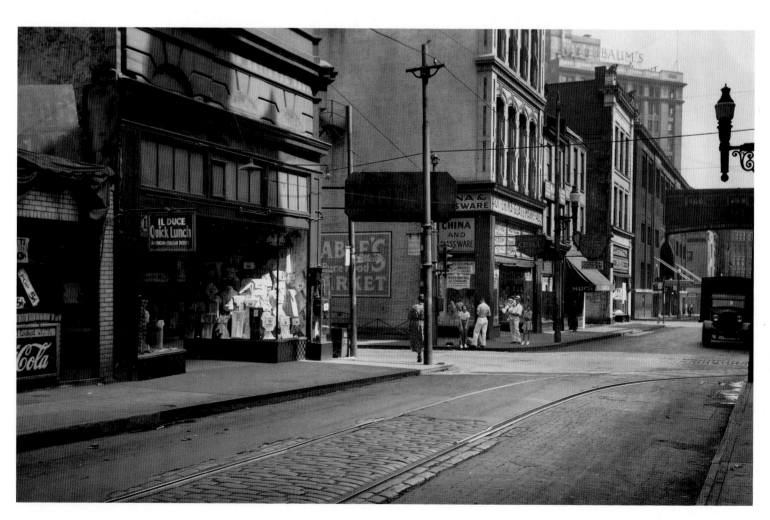

Market Street northeast from number 317. This section of Market Street was absorbed into PPG Place in 1983–84. Fourth Avenue crosses both photographs. In the 1936 photograph there is a small lunchroom on the left called Il Duce Quick Lunch. The name was probably changed when Benito Mussolini, "Il Duce," led Italy into World War II.

Sixth Street south toward Penn Avenue. At the turn of the century there were numerous small hotels such as the Albemarle scattered through the downtown.

Sixth Street from Penn Avenue toward Liberty Avenue.
The former Loew's Penn Theater was transformed into Heinz
Hall in 1971, while across the street, Rosenbaum's Depart-
ment Store was replaced with a parking garage.

Liberty Avenue southwest from Market Street. The lower
Triangle, the area west of Sixth and Market streets, has been
almost totally reconstructed since World War II as part of
Renaissance I and II.

Intersection of Market Street and Liberty Avenue. This site on the corner has contained a retail shop for at least fifty years—only the product has changed from fruit to flowers. The location is a good one, for many pedestrians pass this corner each day.

Liberty Avenue southwest from Fifth Avenue. The Jenkins Arcade was razed in 1983 to make way for Fifth Avenue Place. The buildings beyond it disappeared at the end of the 1940s.

The Wabash Terminal, intersection of Liberty Avenue and Stanwix Street. The Wabash Terminal was one of four imposing turn-of-the-century railroad stations to grace this city. Only two of them have survived. This one was demolished in 1955 to make way for one of the Gateway buildings.

Penn Avenue southwest from Stanwix Street. The vast scale of Renaissance I is revealed in this pair of pictures. In 1933 Penn Avenue extended southwest of Stanwix Street to the Monongahela River. When Gateway Plaza was created during the 1950s, the buildings—and Penn Avenue itself—were demolished.

BRIDGES

1889

■ Among its other labels, Pittsburgh can accurately be called "the city of bridges." Its hilly topography, deeply furrowed by rivers and ravines, has required the building of bridges in many sizes and shapes. Today they usually represent the second, third, or even fourth generation of bridges on those sites. Pittsburgh's bridges, past and present, could amply illustrate a textbook on the evolution of bridge building in America over the past 150 years.

Smithfield Street Bridge. This is Pittsburgh's oldest surviving river bridge, the original span having been built in 1882. It was widened in two stages, first in 1890 and again in 1911. It is the third bridge to span the Monongahela at Smithfield Street. The first, a wooden covered bridge, was built in 1818. It was destroyed by fire in 1845, along with much of the downtown. Its successor was the first wire cable suspension bridge, designed by John Roebling, who later was responsible for the Brooklyn Bridge.

Smithfield Street Bridge. The bridge, including its portals, has remained essentially unchanged since 1911. It is the oldest steel through-truss bridge in America, and the only one in this country employing the over-and-under double-truss construction.

Mount Washington and the Liberty Bridge. There were more major bridges built in Pittsburgh in the second half of the 1920s than during any other five year period in this city's history. Among them was the Liberty Bridge, seen in an early stage of construction in 1926 just upstream from the Pennsylvania Railroad Bridge. The white line across the picture identifies the route of Mount Washington Boulevard (McArdle Roadway), then under construction. The Liberty Tubes also date from the late 1920s. These three projects provided important access roads through and over Mount Washington, enhancing the possibilities of commuting by automobile or bus from the South Hills to the downtown.

Manchester Bridge. The bridges on the Allegheny River are in even greater abundance than on the Monongahela or the Ohio, but the Manchester Bridge is no longer one of them. The architects of the Pittsburgh Renaissance believed that the Point was a better place for a fountain than for the convergence of traffic into the city.

Federal Street and the Sixth Street Bridge. These are the third and fourth bridges to connect Federal Street on the North Side with Sixth Street in the downtown. The two similar buildings shown at the far end of the bridge in 1911 were intended to provide a grand entry into the central city, reminiscent of Roman triumphal arches. The Bessemer Building on the right has been replaced with yet another parking garage, but its partner, the Fulton Building, still stands. In 1927 the old bridge was floated downriver and reconstructed between Coraopolis and Neville Island. Shortly after the new bridge was completed, it received the American Institute of Steel Construction award for the most beautiful bridge built in the United States or Canada in 1928.

Seventh Street Bridge. The new bridges at Seventh and Ninth streets are identical to the Sixth Street Bridge. All three were constructed between 1925 and 1928. In this instance both the old (built in 1885) and the new are suspension bridges. A comparison shows the progress made in suspension bridge design in the intervening forty years.

Pittsburgh, Fort Wayne & Chicago Railroad Bridge. The
earlier bridge was built in the 1850s. By 1904 the Pennsylvania Railroad had absorbed the Pittsburgh, Fort Wayne &
Chicago Railroad and had constructed a new bridge, which
was elevated further in 1918 to accommodate a higher road
bed, designed to carry the railroad above the street level.

Sixteenth Street Bridge. At one time there were ten wooden bridges spanning the three major rivers in and near Pittsburgh. Several of them survived into the early years of this century. After it was originally built in 1838, this bridge underwent major reconstruction several times to repair the damage of fire and flood. Notice the sign above the entrance, which was the standard instruction for such bridges. The present bridge was built in 1923.

Bloomfield Bridge. The Bloomfield Bridge is seen here in the final stages of construction (1914) and reconstruction (1987). The original bridge took four years to build; during its reconstruction it was closed for eight years. Skunk Hollow, the residential area beneath the bridge, was considered an undesirable place in which to live when the bridge was originally built. No one lives there now.

Mission Street Bridge. This modest structure spanning one of the ravines in the hillside south of the Monongahela has changed little in the past fifty years, but the sign, and the horse droppings, have been removed. What makes this worthy of note is that the earlier photograph was taken in 1924, long after the automobile and truck had presumably replaced the horse in domestic and commercial transportation.

■ For close to a century Pittsburgh was the iron and steel manufacturing center of the United States. The effect that this industry had upon the local environment is hard to imagine if one did not experience it in person. The local rivers were lined with a seemingly endless parade of mills and foundries. The sounds and sights and smells that emanated from the river valleys were awesome.

Foundries along the Allegheny. This narrow stretch of flat land between the Allegheny River and the steep hillside on its southern bank was originally called Bayardstown and Croghansville after two prominent citizens of early Pittsburgh. It later became known as the Strip in recognition of its topography. From the 1850s until World War II the Strip District contained Pittsburgh's principal concentration of iron and steel fabricating plants, called foundries. Here iron and steel bars, slabs, and rolls were made into a great variety of products. These foundries have been replaced with wholesale warehouses, diverse commercial and manufacturing enterprises, and a very large parking lot. The Veterans Bridge, opened in 1989, connects the East Street Valley Expressway with the downtown.

IRON & STEEL

1906

Fort Pitt Foundry from Union Station. At the turn of the century many workers lived in close proximity to the mills.

**Fort Pitt Foundry and Sable Iron Works from Union
Station.** Churches in Pittsburgh often served parishes of a
particular ethnic group. St. Philomena's, prominent in the
earlier photograph, served the local residents of German
background. People of Polish and Slovak origin went to
other churches nearby. To say that darkness reigned at noon
in these valleys was not an exaggeration on many days.

Grade crossing, Penn Avenue northeast from Twenty-Eighth Street. Railroad grade crossings were common in the city. In this case the tracks down Penn Avenue are for trolleys; the crossing tracks are a railroad siding to nearby industrial plants.

Painter's Mills, below Duquesne Heights. Painter's Mills,
one of the early basic steel plants of the Carnegie Steel
Company, was located on the south side of the Monongahela
River across from the Point.

Painter's Mills, below Mount Washington. No trace remains of what was an extensive manufacturing operation at the turn of the century.

Jones & Laughlin

IRON & STEEL

Circa 1960

Pittsburgh Works. The Jones & Laughlin mills on the
Monongahela continued to manufacture steel into the 1970s.

Pittsburgh Works on Second Avenue. The addition of the Parkway East and the dismantling of the Jones & Laughlin steel mill have brought major changes to the area of Second Avenue and Bates Street. Only the railroad and Second Avenue are common to both of these photographs separated by forty years.

Boulevard of the Allies exit ramp to Forbes Avenue. The elimination of the mill—and its pollutants—reveals a view of the downtown skyline.

■ Changes in transportation have played a very important role in the evolution and growth of Pittsburgh. First the railroad, then the horse trolley, the incline, the cable car, the electric trolley, the bus, and the automobile have done much to determine where people lived and how they traveled to work. The growth of suburban Pittsburgh was dictated by the location of these various means of transportation. Only the bus and the automobile were not restricted by fixed rails.

Pittsburgh & Lake Erie Railroad Terminal. The Pittsburgh & Lake Erie Railroad Terminal and Freight House were re-born in the 1980s as the Grand Concourse restaurant and Station Square shopping mall—a successful adaptation of old buildings to modern uses.

Pittsburgh & Lake Erie Railroad Terminal. Parking lots and
a new hotel have completed the adaptation of the terminal
to a variety of commercial enterprises.

Northeast from Union Station. The large train shed in the foreground was 556 feet long and 110 feet high. It survived until 1947. These photographs illustrate changes in available modes of transportation. In 1906 there was a multitrack railroad, part of the Pennsylvania main line, crossed by one of Pittsburgh's numerous inclines. Eighty years later the railroad has shrunk and the incline has disappeared, while the addition of the Martin Luther King Busway and the Crosstown Expressway testify to the more recent dominance of the bus and the automobile, with their greater freedom of movement.

Freight yards from the top of Union Station. The mainline tracks (not visible in these photographs) which pass the Union Station still carry considerable freight traffic, but the trains rarely stop. Like those at the Point, the freight yards adjacent to the station have disappeared. The United States Post Office and Courthouse Building, which occupies much of the former freight yard space, was built in 1932.

Twenty-Eighth Street Bridge over the Pennsylvania Railroad, looking west. These comparative views make an eloquent statement of the decline in local railroad activity.

INCLINES

March 1987

Monongahela Incline. The incline, or funicular, is probably the most romantic and interesting means of transportation in the city. Its introduction in the last quarter of the nineteenth century opened up the hilltops to settlement. Though the air was cleaner there, access had previously been too difficult to make residential building practical. Only two inclines remain of more than twenty originally constructed.

Monongahela Incline. In 1915 there were four sets of tracks. Two of them, which have since disappeared, were for the freight incline, which carried horses and wagons with various goods and materials to the top of the bluff.

Penn Incline over Bigelow Boulevard. This incline used to carry passengers and goods from Seventeenth Street in the Strip District to the top of the Hill District. It was dismantled in 1953.

South Hills Junction. Next to the automobile, the electric trolley has probably had a greater impact on local residential patterns than any other means of transportation. Successfully introduced toward the end of the 1880s, trolleys powered by electricity were more efficient in Pittsburgh's hilly terrain than their horse-drawn counterparts. They provided an inexpensive and reliable means of transportation for large numbers of people. By the middle of the 1890s annual ridership numbered in the millions. Streetcar suburbs spread rapidly as suburban living, away from places of employment, became practical. Since 1911 trolleys have converged upon South Hills Junction to pass through the nearby tunnel under Mount Washington.

July 1987

Trolley island at Duquesne Incline, West Carson Street.
Trolley islands used to be a common sight in Pittsburgh.
They posed a traffic hazard for motorists, but made entering
and leaving the trolleys less dangerous for pedestrians.

Fifth Avenue west from Highland Avenue. For several decades horse-drawn vehicles shared the streets of Pittsburgh with trolleys and automobiles. They were a source of irritation for all concerned: the slower pace of the horses impeded automobile traffic, while impatient motorists expressed their displeasure in ways that frightened horses and their apprehensive drivers.

Howe Springs, Fifth Avenue at Highland Avenue. Howe Springs, where thirsty cyclists and others who were passing by might stop for a cool drink of water, was provided by the thoughtfulness of the Howe family, whose house occupied the hilltop beyond. The spring-fed fountain was later enclosed in a pavilion, but potable water has long since ceased to flow.

■ The hillsides of Pittsburgh are littered with steps
for those who like to walk—or have to.

Chestnut Street at Concord Street looking up to Vista
Street, Spring Hill.

STEPS

March 1987

From Pius Street to St. Michael Street, South Side.

Rhine Street steps east from number 1900, Spring Hill.

15 November 1928

STEPS

Rising Main Avenue from the East Street Valley.

Steps from Melrose Avenue to Chautauqua Street, Fineview.

Indian Trail steps from Duquesne Incline to Duquesne Heights. This greatest flight of them all no longer exists.

■ Pittsburgh was, and to some degree still is, a city of distinct, self-contained neighborhoods. This pattern was a consequence of geography, the availability of transportation, and ethnic distinctions, as people of common cultural background chose to live together. First-generation Pittsburghers frequently felt the need for a culturally familiar and supportive environment in a new world that they perceived to be both alien and hostile. Although the reasons for segregation into mutually exclusive communities have diminished, people still live in identifiable neighborhoods, to which they often have long-standing ties of loyalty and affection.

October 1986

Fifth Avenue west from Washington Avenue. Uptown and the lower Hill District were severely altered by Renaissance I, which included the construction of the Civic Arena. Chatham Center, a complex that includes a hotel, condominiums, and offices, was built in 1966.

Smallman Street toward Twenty-First Street. St. Stanislaus
Church has traditionally served a congregation of Polish
background. It was once surrounded by the homes of its
parishioners.

Penn Avenue northeast from opposite number 1715. Produce and other foodstuffs have long been marketed on this stretch of Penn Avenue, close to the wholesale outlets for these goods.

Penn Avenue northeast from number 1723. These stores traditionally spill out onto the pavement to display their wares. In fifty years the general appearance and the marketing techniques of this produce shop have not changed.

Penn Avenue southwest from number 1715. Wholey's fish market is now a fixture on Penn Avenue, but fifty years ago that site was occupied by a wholesale grocer.

August 1986

Butler Street between Fortieth and Forty-First streets.
Shops still line Butler Street, Lawrenceville's main artery, as
it runs parallel to the Allegheny River beyond the Fortieth
Street Bridge. The buildings often date from the nineteenth
century; in this instance their facades have been severely
altered.

■ Many of the eastern suburbs grew on the ridge between the Allegheny and Monongahela rivers. High ground was desirable, away from the worst of the smoke and soot. The railroad, which took a northerly route around the Hill and ran through Shadyside, East Liberty, and Homewood after 1852, accounted for their early growth. Oakland and Squirrel Hill developed rapidly only after 1890, when the electric trolley provided their residents with the transportation necessary to commute to downtown.

Fifth Avenue east from Bigelow Boulevard. Early in the twentieth century the large tract of land bounded by Fifth, Forbes, and Bellefield avenues and Bigelow Boulevard was acquired by Henry Clay Frick with an eye toward development. He never got around to it, and his heirs subsequently sold the land to the University of Pittsburgh as the site for the Cathedral of Learning.

Carnegie Institute and Library, Schenley Plaza. The Carnegie Institute (erected 1892–95) was first housed in a building crowned with twin towers modeled after the campanile in the Piazza of San Marco in Venice. The original building proved to be too small for its varied uses. In 1903–07 it was substantially altered to increase its capacity for books, dinosaurs, and patrons of the arts. The towers disappeared, but the original music hall, which they once flanked, remains.

The Ravine and the Bellefield Bridge from the William Pitt Student Union (formerly the Schenley Hotel). The ravine and bridge in the center of the earlier photograph were obliterated in 1913. The ravine was filled in and the bridge buried with earth taken from the top of Grant's Hill in the downtown, a project called the "removal of the hump." Schenley Plaza was the result.

Schenley Plaza. In 1953 the objective was to maximize the parking possibilities of the plaza. It still serves as a parking lot, but some restraint has been imposed. The landscape architect had intended that the Schenley Fountain be the centerpiece for the plaza, but the construction of the Frick Fine Arts Building (dedicated in 1965) has altered that.

Circa 1905

Phipps Conservatory. The conservatory opened in 1893 and
has continued to offer semiannual flower shows since then.
The old Gothic style entrance was replaced in 1967.

The Duquesne Gardens, Craig Street. The Duquesne Gardens was originally a trolley barn. In 1899 it was converted into an ice skating rink in response to the growing popularity of that sport. Soon it became a sports arena and performance hall. For more than half a century it was the scene of many exciting hockey, basketball, and boxing contests. It was torn down in 1956.

9 June 1937

■ In the 1960s the neighborhood of East Liberty fell victim to the good intentions of the Urban Redevelopment Authority. By the time city planners had finished reorganizing the streets, tearing down the houses, and creating a mall, the area had become so confusing that people tended to avoid East Liberty altogether. This once-flourishing neighborhood that contained six movie houses, Mansmann's Department Store, McCann's Market, and many other retail shops, as well as the Lexington Roller Skating Arena, now struggles to keep its commercial outlets in business.

Penn Avenue east along the 5800 block. Placing a high-rise apartment building across what had been a major traffic artery is one way to baffle the public. The building emphasizes that the street in the foreground was to be open to buses and pedestrians only, although it was subsequently reopened to automobiles as well.

Penn Avenue west from Highland Avenue. This is the
main intersection of East Liberty.

**Intersection of Penn and Frankstown avenues from Shady
Avenue.** On this site only the Liberty Building on the far
left appears to have survived intact.

Frankstown Avenue east from Penn Avenue. Penn Circle
has replaced all of the former buildings and a portion of the
street.

Penn Avenue, south side, between Center and Shady avenues. Where once stood a row of commercial buildings including the Cameraphone Theater, there is now a gigantic bus stop.

Penn Avenue east from number 6101. These comparative photographs speak eloquently of the decline in shopping along this street.

August 1987

Baum Boulevard east from South Beatty Street. On the left is the East Liberty Presbyterian Church, recently completed when the earlier photograph was taken. On the right is the Liberty Market, completed in 1900. Around 1915 it was purchased by the Pittsburgh Sportsmen's Association and renamed Motor Square Garden. For the next quarter of a century it served as a multipurpose arena for a variety of recreational and sports activities. In the four decades after 1940 it housed a Cadillac agency. In April 1988 the renovated building, renamed Motor Square Garden, reopened as a modern day version of . . . a market house.

November 1986

Highland Avenue south from Margaretta Street. Traffic blinkers, a common sight in the 1930s, constituted a formidable traffic hazard. They were usually set in concrete and placed in the center of the street. Highland Avenue beyond Penn Circle has some earlier buildings intact, including the Sears, Roebuck store which opened in 1929. The portion of Margaretta Street, from which the earlier photograph was taken, has disappeared to make room for East Liberty Boulevard, a route that enables motorists to bypass the East Liberty business district.

Lincoln Avenue from Frankstown Avenue. Today we lament the potholes that proliferate on our streets, but few would argue that the old paving stones and trolley tracks would be an improvement.

Reynolds Street east from Lang Avenue. The Frick Park Market has occupied this site since 1942. Prior to that the building housed the Lang Drug Store in the 1920s and early 1930s and an A & P store in the later 1930s. But eighty years ago it was a "mom and pop" grocery store, just as it is today.

Reynolds Street at Homewood Avenue looking east. In 1934 the imposing entrance to Frick Park was under construction. Also in the 1930s the city undertook a major tree-planting effort. The results can be seen today.

November 1986

South Negley Avenue north from Fair Oaks Street. Squirrel
Hill developed as a streetcar suburb later than the railroad
suburbs of Shadyside, East Liberty, and Homewood. As late
as 1909 even so important a street as Negley Avenue
remained unpaved.

Junction Hollow, Saline Valley. The point from which the photographs were taken is the same; the subject area is the same; but there is a difference! When the Parkway East was constructed, it wrought significant changes in at least this perspective of the Saline Valley. The lower photograph shows what you would see if you could look beyond the Parkway.

15 June 1937

■ Allegheny City was not incorporated into the city of Pittsburgh until 1907. By then that area north of the Allegheny and the Ohio rivers had a population of 150,000. Topographically, it was composed of several ridges separated by steep, narrow valleys which ran at right angles to the rivers and ended in the flatland along the riverbanks. The broad flat area across from the Point became the center of Allegheny City, while the ridge tops and intervening valleys became separate neighborhoods: Troy Hill, Spring Garden, Spring Hill, East Street Valley, Fineview, and Perry Hilltop, among others. Allegheny City has a rich and interesting history of diversified industry, elegant living, distinguished citizens, and local lore which focuses particularly upon that large segment of the population which was of German extraction.

Federal Street looking north. Allegheny Center was constructed in the 1960s, drastically changing the center of Old Allegheny. The new mall sits astride Federal Street, once the main north-south artery.

Federal Street looking south from the corner opposite the Market House. More than five hundred buildings were razed to convert this old section of the city into a shopping mall.

The Market House, Federal Street. The old market building, constructed in 1863, was torn down in 1966.

August 1987

Carnegie Library across Diamond Park. The Carnegie Library and Performance Hall was constructed in 1889, the gift of Andrew Carnegie to the neighborhood in which he spent his youth. The building remains as a landmark and reference point.

April 1987

West Lacock Street west from Cremo Street. The river-
front, once an industrial belt, freight yard, and modest
residential area, has undergone—and continues to
undergo—dramatic changes. This neighborhood of houses
and small shops has given way to elevated highways and
Three Rivers Stadium.

North Avenue west from Buena Vista Street. Some buildings along North Avenue above Allegheny Center have disappeared, although time has dealt more gently with this area, which includes the Mexican War streets.

■ The next five pairs of photographs portray examples of residential housing that have survived but changed their outer surfaces while doing so. Housing in Pittsburgh is generally constructed of either wood or brick. Wooden frame houses can last for a long time if they are carefully maintained, but such upkeep requires frequent, expensive attention. The solution to reducing exterior maintenance was first found by using various types of fiber siding, followed by aluminum and plastic siding, which now sheathes practically all the surviving frame houses in the city. Modern siding is almost maintenance-free and has a clean, polished look, but one may still lament the disappearance of the texture of the wood that it covers. Also gone are many of the wooden porches, balustrades, shutters, eaves, and trim with their ornamental bric-a-brac, replaced with cement, iron, and aluminum that is functional and durable but not nearly as pleasing to the eye.

Rhine Street at Wessner Street. The once attractive building in the center, which served as a corner grocery store, has been covered with fiber shingles.

2527 Spring Garden Avenue.

2713 Spring Garden Avenue.

232

2801 and 2807 Veteran Street (off Perrysville Avenue).

234

1909 Perrysville Avenue. In the 1926 photograph this large house appears to have been made of brick, but it is actually a frame house which was then covered with insulbrick, and subsequently with aluminum siding.

February 1987

Perrysville Avenue at Perryview Avenue. Here is an attractive house seen in 1928 just after it was built. In 1976–77 the state of Pennsylvania required the owners to sell the property to the Department of Transportation to become the right-of-way for a road. The house was torn down at that time, but the road was never built.

Cutler Street west from Perrysville Avenue. Cutler Street traverses an intimidating hillside, which did not deter the builders of a row of houses and a flight of steps.

Cutler Street east from Wilson Avenue. Whether or not the street was rougher before or after it was paved with Belgian blocks is open to conjecture. The open porches have been closed off by a succession of awnings, perhaps an indication of a decline in neighborliness.

824 and 830 Beech Avenue. As a consequence of the Allegheny West and Manchester renovations, these two buildings have been preserved and spruced up. Externally they are little altered from the way they looked sixty years ago.

California Avenue from Kleber Street. These buildings are generally the same as they were more than sixty years ago, but the condition of the streets has vastly improved.

Kleber Street from California Avenue.

Beaver Avenue southeast from Columbus Avenue. Of this
once commercial intersection only the corner curb on the
right remains.

EAST STREET VALLEY

February 1989

East Street from Brahm Street steps. The construction of highways for suburban commuters can have devastating effects upon residential areas that happen to be in the way. The residents fought a long, but unsuccessful, battle to save their homes in the East Street Valley.

Harry C. Smith's Meat Market, 1424 East Street. Mr.
Smith or his heir had probably been forced out of business by
the competition of the supermarkets long before the highway
came along.

OLD BIRMINGHAM

5 November 1926

■ Even more than its northern counterpart, the South Side offers a formidable challenge to residential development and urban expansion. The narrow strip of land along the Monongahela and Ohio rivers was occupied by glass factories soon after Pittsburgh was settled; after the middle of the nineteenth century most of the glass works were crowded out by iron and steel mills. The workers lived among the mills, but the area was noisome and overcrowded. Builders further from the river were confronted with an intimidating hillside, high and steep. They were not deterred, and houses soon began to appear, terraced up the hill. This was desirable housing, somewhat removed from the industrial noise, smoke, and dirt in the valley below.

1100 block of East Carson Street. Carson Street was, and is, the main street of this neighborhood. The Iron and Glass Bank building had just been completed when the earlier photograph was taken.

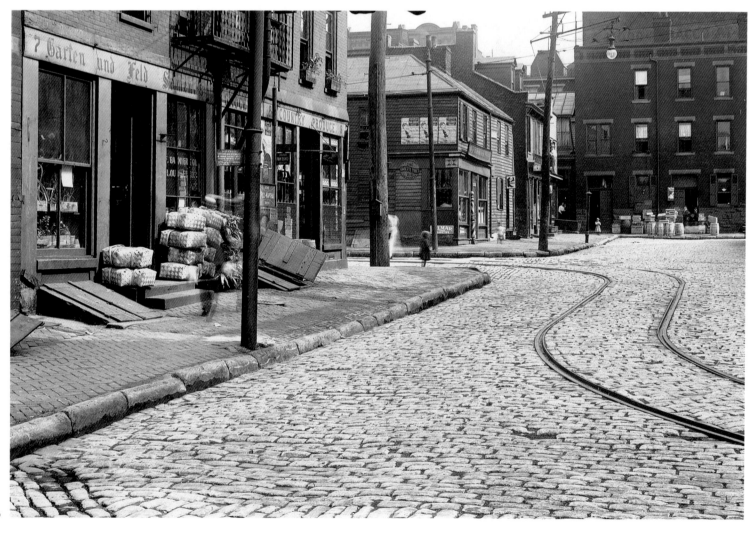

The north side of Market House Square. Retail stores, including a German feed and seed store, clustered in a square around the South Side Market House. The retail functions of this square have largely disappeared, and the market house is now a service and recreation center for senior citizens.

1720 East Carson Street. Livery stables were a common sight in nineteenth-century Pittsburgh, but they have long since disappeared. Frequently the livery stable operator did double duty as an undertaker. The further removed we are from the age of horse transportation, the more nostalgic we may become about it, forgetting that it certainly had its inconvenient side.

Wachter Street at South Eighteenth Street. By 1911 the houses on this street appeared substantially as they do today.

Josephine Street below Telescope Street. Sometimes the streets wind up the hillside like goat trails, seeking the easiest route. The houses perch wherever a bit of usable space can be found. A careful examination of these photographs reveals that virtually all of the buildings of 1925 remain essentially intact.

East Warrington Avenue west from St. Thomas Street.
Sometimes the streets go straight up the hillside, creating a
steep ascent, with the houses terraced accordingly. This
particular row of frame houses has undergone a considerable
transformation in fifty years, thanks to various forms of
exterior siding.

Upper Shelly Street looking west from the circle. Another way to adapt housing to a hilly terrain is to have the streets run along the face of the hill. In a few instances, such as this, they are split-level streets.

Upper Shelly Street looking east. This is a well-preserved stretch of the street viewed from the opposite end.

Backs of houses on Sterling Street viewed from the Mission Street Bridge. The backs of these houses provide an interesting example of continuity and change.

Arlington Avenue east from number 2818. Even in 1924 there were plenty of unpaved streets within the city of Pittsburgh. Many areas still had that "country look."

Becks Run Road northeast from number 819. Before driveways were needed for private automobiles, a footbridge could provide access to the house.

760 to 732 Brookline Boulevard from Flatbush Avenue. In 1933 the trolleys ran down the middle of Brookline Boulevard on their own separate right-of-way. What remains is a very wide street, one of the few streets in the city that is wide enough to permit head-in parking. The buildings of half-a-century ago look much as they did then and still house retail shops along a neighborhood street.

Shiloh and Sycamore streets. Freyvogel's Drug Store is gone, but the street still serves as a neighborhood shopping center.

Grandview Avenue at Plymouth Street. The building that once housed Butler's Grocery Store now stands in the shadow of the Trimont Tower. Apparently a beer distributorship has little use for windows.

Kramer Way east of Boggs Avenue. The back of Mount Washington descends more gradually than its precipitous front, allowing for the development of a considerable residential area that does not appear to be clinging to the hillside. Here there are a number of interesting streets that have changed little through the years.

Plymouth Street toward Sycamore Street from number 313.
In these photographs only the different vintage of automobile
and the Trimont Tower in the distance mark the passage of
time.

Grandview Avenue east from number 1632. Along the Duquesne Heights portion of Grandview Avenue this unprepossessing frame house now shares the view with the new highrise condominiums.

West Carson Street west from Glenmawr Avenue. Along this open stretch of Carson Street traffic moves at a rapid pace. Even in 1911 the policeman was not above hiding behind a building so that he might trot out and nab an unsuspecting speeder.

August 1986

Chartiers Avenue north from Allendale Street, Sheraden Park. The pharmacy on the corner has occupied the same building since 1892. The sign over the door proclaims, "still a drug store."

In the 1920s and 1930s many neighborhoods were served by the Atlantic and Pacific Tea Company grocery chain. These were not the modern super-markets that we know, but modest stores that differed little from the "mom and pop" grocery stores with which they competed. In the next three sets of photographs the modern appearance of the buildings would not lead one to suspect that they had ever been occupied by a grocery store. In the fourth, the entire block of buildings has disappeared.

A & P STORES

3197 Chartiers Avenue at Kelvin Street.

Rhine Street between Horloge and Yetta streets.

3100 block of West Carson Street.

1400 block of Lincoln Avenue west from Lemington
Avenue.

■ By the turn of the century the development of basic industries in Pittsburgh had created great fortunes for those who owned and managed them, and those who invested in them. These people built palatial mansions in Allegheny West and in the eastern suburbs of Oakland, Shadyside, Highland Park, Homewood, and Point Breeze. These houses were frequently set in spacious grounds, and their flamboyant styles were intended to advertise the newly acquired wealth of their owners. Only a few of these extravagant houses remain. The houses themselves became impractical, as family size declined and domestic service became less available. Another contributing factor to their demise was the great value of the large tracts of land on which they stood.

Henry Oliver's residence, 845 Ridge Avenue. Several other houses along Ridge Avenue have been adapted for academic use by the Community College of Allegheny County, but this house was replaced by a large institutional structure.

Christopher Magee's residence, Forbes Avenue and Halket Street. Christopher Magee was the political boss and mayor of Pittsburgh for the last two decades of the nineteenth century. The property subsequently became the location for Magee-Women's Hospital.

Charles Lockhart's residence, North Highland Avenue south of St. Marie Street. The Pittsburgh Theological Seminary now occupies the site of this stately home.

"Woodmont," Charles C. Scaife's residence, 1136 Western Avenue. The lot where this mansion once stood is now the site of several sprawling commercial buildings.

"Cairncarque," Robert Pitcairn's residence, southeast corner of the intersection of Ellsworth and Amberson avenues. The spacious grounds of this house were used by a housing developer to build numerous residences on Pitcairn Place (above) and on Amberson Avenue (below).

Colonel James M. Guffey's residence, Fifth Avenue between Morewood and Amberson avenues. Here one mansion has been replaced with another—but in 1984 the house was converted into several condominiums.

■ The division of large houses into separate apartments has occurred in a few instances, but more commonly the old mansion was demolished to make way for a variety of new structures, often of a nondescript nature, that house apartments or condominiums, thereby maximizing the utilization of the property.

Jacob Gusky's residence, 5506 Fifth Avenue.

W. Harry Brown's residence, 5742 Fifth Avenue.

The house is gone—I know not where;
Might it have vanished in thin air?

F. W. McKee's residence, northeast corner of the intersection of Fifth and Highland avenues.

Did it fall prey to fire or theft,
Leaving its family bereft?

SHADYSIDE

Circa 1889

Mary B. Hailman's residence, Shady Lane (Avenue).

Or fated to sedate decline,
Victim of ravages of time?

HIGHLAND PARK

February 1987

Southwest corner of Stanton and Highland avenues.

How sad to be judged obsolete,
When once the pride of the elite.

Circa 1905

■ Some photographic essays conclude with a dramatic finish—a brilliant sunset or a spectacular overview. Obviously that is not the case with this work. We celebrate what Pittsburgh has become and what it is becoming, and rightly so. Much of the past has been saved and enhanced, while much that is modern is both stylish and visually satisfy-

ing. But it is well to remember that change is not always progress, at least in the visual sense. Since many of the pairs of photographs in this book have illustrated that observation, it is appropriate that we end these comparisons with a stately home that has been replaced by . . . Jake's Bar.

George Lauder's residence, 7403 Penn Avenue.

Photo Credits

All of the "Now" photographs were taken by the author. Sources of the "Then" photographs are as follows.

Pittsburgh City Photographer Collection, Archives of Industrial Society, University of Pittsburgh: 16, 30, 32, 34, 36, 38, 40, 48, 50, 52, 56, 58, 70, 72, 74, 78, 80, 82, 84, 88, 94, 96, 98, 108, 116, 126, 136, 144, 146, 148, 154, 156, 158, 162, 164, 166, 168, 170, 172, 174, 180, 188, 190, 192, 194, 196, 198, 200, 202, 204, 208, 210, 214, 216, 218, 220, 222, 224, 226, 228, 230, 232, 234, 236, 238, 240, 242, 244, 246, 248, 250, 252, 254, 256, 260, 262, 264, 266, 268, 272, 274, 276, 278, 280, 282, 284, 286, 288, 292, 294, 298, 304, 320.

Pittsburgh Photographic Library, Carnegie Library of Pittsburgh: 4 (photo by Frank E. Bingaman), 14 (gift of Allegheny Conference on Community Development), 22 (gift of Harry B. Johnston), 28, 44, 46, 54 (photo by Frank E. Bingaman), 62, 64 (gift of Mrs. E. L. Oschman), 66 (photo by Frank E. Bingaman), 68, 76, 100, 102, 104, 112 (photo by A. M. Brown), 114 (photo by A. M. Brown), 118 (gift of Harry B. Johnston), 120 (gift of Harry B. Johnston), 124 (photo by Todd Webb for Standard Oil of New Jersey), 132 (photo by A. M. Brown), 134, 138, 142, 150, 152 (photo by Luke Swank), 160 (photo by Harold Corsini), 176 (gift of the University of Pittsburgh Press), 182 (photo by Harold Corsini), 206, 212, 258, 270 (photo by Clyde Hare), 290 (photo by A. M. Brown), 296, 300 (gift of Richard L. Linder), 306, 312 (gift of Richard L. Linder), 314 (photo from *Pittsburg Bulletin*, vol. 49).

Allegheny Conference on Community Development: 2, 186.

Historical Society of Western Pennsylvania (postcards): 6, 60, 86, 178, 184.

Wonday Film Service (postcards): 8 (photo by Sid Lane), 10, 122 (photo by Sid Lane).

Gazette-Times, *Story of Pittsburgh* (1908): 12.

Fortune (August 1967): 18.

Art Work of Pittsburg (1899): 20.

Pittsburgh Art Commission: 24, 92.

The Pittsburgh Plan (1924): 26.

H. R. Page & Co., *Pittsburgh Illustrated* (1889): 42, 302, 316, 318.

Pittsburgh and Allegheny (1889): 90.

Pittsburgh Architectural Club: Exhibition (1914): 106.

Allegheny Observatory Collection, Archives of Industrial Society, University of Pittsburgh: 110.

Harold H. McLean, *Pittsburgh and Lake Erie Railroad* (1980): 128, 130.

Folding View Book of Pittsburgh (1915): 140.

Robert M. Palmer, *Pictorial Pittsburgh* (1905): 308, 310, 322.